Code Of Canon Law

Canon 66 «The Christian economy, therefore, since it is the new and definitive Covenant, will never pass away; and no new public revelation is to be expected before the glorious manifestation of our Lord Jesus Christ." Yet even if Revelation is already complete, it has not been made completely explicit; it remains for Christian faith gradually to grasp its full significance over the course of the centuries.

Canon 67 Throughout the ages, there have been so-called «private» revelations, some of which have been recognized by the authority of the Church. They do not belong, however, to the deposit of faith. It is not their role to improve or complete Christ's definitive Revelation, but to help live more fully by it in a certain period of history. Guided by the Magisterium of the Church, the sensus fidelium knows how to discern and welcome in these revelations whatever constitutes an authentic call of Christ or his saints to the Church.

Christian faith cannot accept "revelations" that claim to surpass or correct the Revelation of which Christ is the fulfilment, as is the case in certain non-Christian religions and also in certain recent sects which base themselves on such "revelations."

The Full of Grace:

The Early Years.

The Merit.

Joseph's Passion.

The Blue Angel.

The Boyhood of Jesus.

Follow Me:

Treasure with 7 Names

Where there are Thorns, there also will be roses

For Love that Perseveres

The Apostolic College

The Decalogue

The Chronicles of Jesus & Judas Iscariot:

I See You As You Are

Those who are Marked

Jesus Weeps

Lazarus:

That Beautiful Blonde

Flowers of Bounty

Claudia Procula:

Do You Love the Nazarene?

The Caprice of Court Morals

Christian Tenets:

On Reincarnation

Mary of Magdala:

Ah! My Beloved! I Reached You At Last!

Lamb Books
Illustrated adaptations for the whole family

LAMB BOOKS

Published by Lamb Books, 2 Dalkeith Court, 45 Vincent Street, London SW1P 4HH;
UK, USA, FR, IT, SP, PT, DE

www.lambbooks.org

First published by Lamb Books 2013
This edition
001

The author and publisher are grateful to the Centro Editoriale Valtoriano in Italy for Permission to quote from the Poem of the Man- God by Maria Valtorta, by Valtorta Publishing

Set in Bookman Old Style R
Printed and bound by CPI Group (UK) Ltd, Croydon, CR0, 4YY

The **Chronicles** Of **Jesus** & **Judas** **Iscariot**

I See You As You Are

LAMBBOOKS

Acknowledgements

The material in this book is adapted from 'The Poem of the Man+God' (The Gospel As Revealed To Me) by Maria Valtorta, first approved by Pope Pius XII in 1948, when, in a meeting on February 26th 1948, witnessed by three other priests, he ordered the three priest present to "Publish this work as it is".

In 1994, the Vatican heeded to the calls of Christians worldwide and have begun to examine the case for the Canonization of Maria Valtorta (Little John).

The Poem of the Man God was described by Pope Pius' confessor as "edifying". Mystical revelations have long been the province of priests and the religious. Now, they are accessible to all. May all who read this adaptation, also find it edifying. And through this light, may Faith be renewed.

Special Thanks to the Centro Editoriale Valtortiano in Italy for permission to quote from the Poem of the Man God by Maria Valtorta, nick named, Little John.

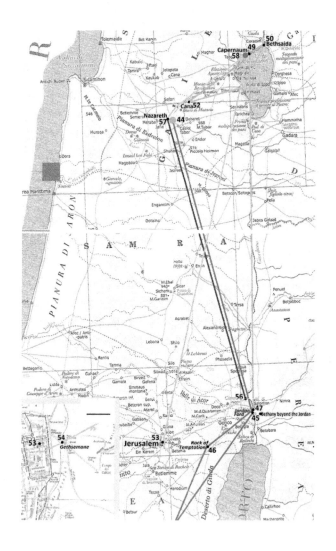

"Judas investigates, quibbles, is obstinate, even when he pretends to give in he still has mental reservations. John feels he is nothing, he accepts everything, he does not ask for reasons, he is satisfied with making Me happy. That is the example."

Jesus. 4th January 1945-' The Gospel As Revealed To Me' by Maria Valtorta,

Jesus Meets Judas Iscariot And Thomas And Cures Simon The Zealot.

It is evening time during Passover and the town of Jerusalem is crowded with pilgrims hurrying home. Jesus with His six disciples, walk towards the country house set among the thick olive trees, where He is a guest. Judas Thaddeus, who had wanted to come to Jerusalem with Jesus, is not present.

From the rustic open space in front of the house, A terraced hill covered in olive trees slopes down to a little water torrent flowing along a valley formed by two hills at the top of which there is the Temple on the one whilst the other is covered only with olive trees. Jesus has just begun to climb up the peaceful slope of the hill of olive trees when an elderly man, possibly the farmer or owner of the olive grove approaches the group and addresses himself to John, his manner familiar.

'John, there are two men awaiting your friend.'

'Where are they? Who are they? '

'I don't know. One is certainly Judaean. The other... I don't know. I didn't ask him.'

'Where are they?'

'In the kitchen, waiting, and... and... yes... there is another man who is all covered with sores. I made him stay over there, because I am afraid he may be a leper. He says he wants to see the Prophet Who spoke in the Temple.'

Jesus, Who has been silent, says: 'Let us go to him first. Tell the others to come if they so wish. I will speak to them there, in the olive-grove.

'And He makes for the place indicated by the man.

'And what about us? What shall we do? 'Asks Peter.

'Come, if you want.'

A man, muffled up, is leaning against the rustic wall supporting the terrace nearest to the property boundary. He must have reached it via a path along the torrent. When he sees Jesus approaching him, he shouts: 'Go back. Back! Have mercy on me!' And he bares his trunk dropping his tunic to the ground. His face is covered with scabs but his trunk is one big sore that in places have become deep wounds, some of which look like burns whilst others are whitish and glossy, as if there is a thin white pane of glass on them.

'Are you a leper? What do you want of Me? '

'Don't curse me! Don't stone me. I have been told that the other evening You revealed Yourself as the

Voice of God and the Bearer of Grace. I was also told that You gave assurance that by raising Your Sign, You will cure all diseases. Please raise it on me. I have come from the sepulchres... over there... I crept like a snake amongst the bushes near the torrent to arrive here without being seen. I waited until evening before leaving because at dusk it is more difficult to see who I am. I dared... I found this man, the man of the house, he is good. He did not kill me. He only said: "Wait over there, near the little wall." Have mercy on me.'

Jesus goes nearer to the leper but the six disciples together with the landlord and the two strangers stay far back and look disgusted.

'Don't come nearer. Don't! I am infected!' cries the
leper but Jesus comes closer still. He looks at the
leper so mercifully, that the man begins to cry and
kneeling down with his face almost touching the
ground, he moans: 'Your Sign! Your Sign!'

'It will be raised when it is time. But now I say to you: Stand up. Be healed. I want it. And be the sign in this town that must recognize Me. Rise, I say. And do not sin, out of gratitude to God!'
Slowly, the man rises, seeming to emerge from the long flowery grass as from a shroud... and is healed. He looks at himself in the last dim light of the day. He is healed. He shouts:

'I am clean! Oh! What shall I do for You now?'

'You must comply with the Law. Go to the priest. Be good in future. Go.'

The man is about to throw himself at Jesus' feet, but remembering that he is still unclean according to the Law, restrains himself and instead kisses his own hand, and throws a kiss to Jesus and weeps. He weeps out of joy.

The others are dumbfounded.

Jesus turns away from the healed man and rouses them smiling. 'My friends, it was only leprosy of the flesh. But you will see leprosy fall from hearts. Is it you that wanted Me? 'He asks the two strangers. 'Here I am. Who are you?'

'We heard You the other evening... in the Temple. We looked for You in town. A man, who said he is a relative of Yours, told us You stay here.'

'Why are you looking for Me?'

'To follow You, if You will allow us, because You have words of truth.'

'Follow Me? But do you know where I am going?'

'No, Master, but certainly to glory.'

'Yes. But not to a glory of this world. I am going to a glory which is in Heaven and is conquered by virtue and sacrifice. Why do you want to follow Me?' He asks them again.

'To take part in Your glory.'

'According to Heaven?'

'Yes, according to Heaven.'

'Not everybody is able to arrive there because Mammon lays more snares for those who yearn for Heaven than for the rest. And only he who has strong will power can resist. Why follow Me, if to follow Me would mean a continuous struggle against the enemy, which is in us, against the hostile world, and against the Enemy who is Satan?'

'Because that is the desire of our souls, which have been conquered by You. You are holy and powerful. We want to be Your friends.'

'Friends!!!' Jesus is silent and sighs. Then He stares at the one who has been the spokesman and who has now removed the mantle-hood from his head, and is bareheaded. 'Who are you? You speak better than a man of the people.'

'I am Judas, the son of Simon. I come from Kerioth. But I am of the Temple. I am waiting for and dreaming of the King of the Jews. I heard You speak like a king. I saw Your kingly gestures. Take me with You.'

16

'Take you? Now? At once? No.'

'Why not, Master?'

'Because it is better to examine ourselves carefully before venturing on very steep roads.'

'Do You not believe I am sincere?'

'You have said it. I believe in your impulsiveness. But I do not believe in your perseverance. Think about it, Judas. I am going away now and I will be back for Pentecost. If you are in the Temple, you will see Me. Examine yourself. And who are you? '.

'I am another one who saw You. I would like to be with You. But now I am frightened. '

'No. Presumption ruins people. Fear may be an impediment, but it is a help when it originates from humility. Do not be afraid. Think about it, too, and when I come back... '

'Master, You are so holy! I am afraid of not being worthy. Nothing else. Because I do not doubt my love... '

'What is your name? '

'Thomas, of Didymus. '

'I will remember your name. Go in peace. '

Jesus dismisses them and He goes into the hospitable house for supper.

The six disciples with Him want to know many things. 'Why, Master, why did You treat them differently? Because there was a difference. Both of them had the same impulsiveness... 'Asks John.

'My friend, also the same impulsiveness may have a different taste and bring about a different effect. They both certainly had the same impulsiveness. But they were not the same in their purpose. And the one who appears less perfect is, in fact, more perfect, because he has no incentive to human glory. He loves Me because he loves Me. '

'And so do I. '

'And I, too. ', 'And I. ', 'And I. ', 'And I. ', 'And I. '

'I know. I know you for what you are. '

'Are we therefore perfect? '

'Oh! No! But, like Thomas, you will become perfect if you persevere in your desire to love. Perfect?! Oh! My friends! And who is perfect but God? '

'You are! '

'I solemnly tell you that I am not perfect by Myself, if you think I am a prophet. No man is perfect. But I am perfect because He Who is speaking to you is the Word of the Father: part of God. His thought that becomes Word. I have Perfection in Myself. And you must believe Me to be such if you believe that I am the Word of the Father. And yet, see, My friends, I want to be called the Son of man because I lower Myself taking upon Myself all the miseries of man, to bear them as My first scaffold, and cancel them, after bearing them, without suffering from them Myself. What a burden, My friends! But I bear it with joy. It is a joy for Me to bear it, because, since I am the Son of mankind, I will make mankind once again the child of God. As it was on the first day. '

Jesus speaks very gently, sitting at the poor table, gesticulating calmly with His hands on the table, His head slightly inclined to one side, His face lit up from below by a small oil lamp on the table. He smiles gently, He Who shortly before, was so majestic a Master in His bearing, is now friendly in His gestures. His disciples listen to Him closely.

'Master... why did Your cousin not come, even though he knows where You live?'

'My Peter!... You will be one of My stones, the first one. But not all the stones can be easily used. Have you seen the marble blocks in the Praetorium building? With hard labour they were torn away from the bosom of the mountain side, and are now part of the Praetorium. Look instead at those stones down there shining in the moonlight, in the water of the Kidron. They arrived in the river- bed by themselves, and if anyone wants to take them, they do not put up any resistance. My cousin is like the first stones I am speaking of... The bosom of the mountain side: his family, they contend for him with Me. '

'But I want to be exactly like the stones in the torrent. I am quite prepared to

Leave everything for You: home, wife, fishing, brothers. Everything, Rabboni, for You. '

'I know, Peter. That is why I love you. Also Judas will come. '

'Who? Judas of Kerioth? I don't care for him. He is a dandy young man, but... I prefer... I myself prefer... 'They all laugh at Peter's witty remark. '... There is nothing to laugh at. I mean that I prefer a sincere Galilean, a rough fisherman, but without any fraud to... to townsfolk who... I don't know... here: the Master knows what I mean. '

'Yes, I know. But do not judge. We need one another in this world; the good are mixed with the wicked, just like flowers in a field. Hemlock grows beside the salutary mallow. '

'I would like to ask one thing... '

'What, Andrew? '

'John told me about the miracle You worked at Cana... We were hoping so much that You would work one at Capernaum... and You said that You would not work any miracles before fulfilling the Law. Why Cana then? And why here and not in Your own fatherland? '

'To obey the Law is to be united to God and that increases our capabilities. A miracle is the proof of the union with God, as well as of God's benevolent and assenting presence. That is why I wanted to perform My duty as an Israelite, before starting the series of miracles. '

'But You were not bound to fulfil the Law. '

'Why? As the Son of God, I was not. But as a son of the Law, yes, I was. For the time being, Israel knows Me only as such... and, even later, almost everyone in Israel will know Me as such, nay, even less. But I do not want to scandalize Israel and therefore I obey the Law. '

'You are holy. '

'Holiness does not bar obedience. Nay it makes obedience perfect. Besides everything else, there is a good example to be given. What would you say of a father, of an elder brother, of a teacher, of a priest who did not give good examples? '

'And what about Cana? '

'Cana was to make My Mother happy. Cana is the advance due to My Mother. She anticipates Grace. Here I honour the Holy City, making her, in public, the starting point of My power as Messiah. But there, at Cana, I paid honour to the Holy Mother of God, Full of Grace. The world received Me through Her. It is only fair that My first miracle in the world should be for Her. '

There is a knocking at the door then, Thomas returning, enters and throws himself at Jesus' feet.

'Master... I cannot wait until You come back. Let me come with You. I am full of faults, but I have my love, my only real great treasure. It is Yours, it's for You. Let me come, Master... '

Jesus lays His hand on Thomas' head. 'You may stay, Didymus. Follow Me. Blessed are those who are sincere and persistent in their will. You are all blessed. You are more than relatives to Me, because you are My children and My brothers, not according to the blood that dies but according to the will of God and to your spiritual wishes. Now I tell you that I have no closer relative than those

21

who do the will of My Father, and you do it because you want what is good. '

The Iscariot Finds Jesus At Gethsemane And Is Accepted As A Disciple.

It is evening, turning dark and the daylight grows fainter and fainter in the thick olive-grove where, Jesus, alone, is sitting on one of the little ground terraces, in His familiar posture; His elbows resting on His knees, His forearms forward and His hands joined. He has taken off His mantle as though He were warm, and His white tunic stands out against the green of the surroundings made even darker by the twilight.

A man approaches through the olive-trees and seems to be looking for something or someone. He is tall, and his garments gay: of a yellow pink hue that makes his big mantle more flamboyant, adorned as it is with swinging fringes. His face is somewhat obscured by the dim light and the distance, and also because the edge of his mantle falls over part of his face. When he sees Jesus, he makes a gesture as if to say: 'There He is! 'And he hastens his step. When he is a few meters away, he greets Him: 'Hail, Master! '

Jesus turns round suddenly and looks up,
because the man is standing on the next terrace,
which is higher up. Jesus looks at him, His
expression serious and also sad. The man says
again: 'I greet You, Master. I am Judas of Kerioth.
Do You not recognize me? Do You not remember? '

'I remember and recognize you. You spoke to Me here with Thomas, last Passover. '

'And You said to me: "Think about it and make up your mind before I come back." I have made up my mind. I will come. '

'Why are you coming, Judas? 'Jesus is really sad.

'Because... The last time I told You why. Because I dream of the Kingdom of Israel and I see You as a king. '

'Is that why you are coming? '

'Yes, it is. I will put myself and everything I possess: capability, acquaintances, friends, and fatigue at Your service and at the service of Your mission to rebuild Israel. '

The two, now close, standing face to face, stare at each other; Jesus is grave and melancholy. Judas, exalted by his dream, is smiling, handsome, young, sprightly and ambitious.

'I did not look for you, Judas. '

'I know. But I looked for You. For days and days I have been putting people at the gates to warn me of Your arrival. I thought You would be coming with followers and would therefore be easy to notice. Instead... I understood that You had been here, because a group of pilgrims was blessing You because You had cured a sick man. But no one could tell me where You were. Then I remembered this place. And I have come. If I had not found You here, I would have resigned myself to not finding You any more... '

'Do you think it is a good thing for you, that you found Me? '

'Yes, because I was looking for You. I was longing for You, I want You. '

'Why? Why did you look for Me? '

'But I have told You, Master! Did You not understand? '

'I did understand you. Yes, I did. But I want you also to understand Me before you follow Me. Come. We will walk and talk. 'And they start walking, one beside the other, up and down the paths that criss-cross in the olive- grove. 'You want to follow Me for a human reason, Judas. But I must dissuade you. I have not come for that. '

'But are You not the designated King of the Jews? The one of whom the Prophets spoke? Others have come. But they lacked too many things and they fell like leaves no longer supported by the wind. But You have God with You, in fact You work miracles. Where there is God, the success of the mission is guaranteed. '

'You have spoken the truth. I have God with Me. I am His Word. I was prophesied by the Prophets, promised to the Patriarchs, expected by the people. But why, Israel, have you become so blind and deaf that you are no longer able to read and see, to hear and understand the reality of events? My

Kingdom is not of this world, Judas. Allow yourself to be convinced of that. I have come to Israel to bring Light and Glory. But not the light and glory of the earth. I have come to call the just of Israel to the Kingdom. Because it is from Israel that the plant of eternal life is to come, and with Israel it is to be formed, the plant, the sap of which will be the Blood of the Lord, the plant that will spread all over the earth, until the end of time. My first followers will be from Israel. My first confessors will be from Israel. But also My persecutors will be from Israel. Also My executioners will be from Israel. And also My traitor will Be from Israel... '

'No, Master. That will never happen. If everyone should betray You, I will remain with You and defend You.'

'You, Judas? And on what do you base your certainty?'

'On my honour as a man.'

'Which is more fragile than a cobweb, Judas. It is God we have to ask for the strength to be honest and faithful. Man!... Man accomplishes human deeds. To accomplish spiritual deeds – and to follow the Messiah with truthfulness and justice is to accomplish a spiritual deed – it is necessary to kill man and make him be born again. Are you capable of so much?'

'Yes, Master. And in any case... Not everybody in Israel will love You. But Israel will not give the Messiah executioners and traitors. Israel has been waiting for You for centuries! '

'I will be given them. Remember the Prophets...
Their words... and their end. I am destined to
disappoint many. And you are one of them. Judas,
you have here in front of you a mild, peaceful poor
man, who wishes to remain poor. I have not come
to impose Myself and make war. I am not going to
contend with the strong and mighty ones for any
kingdom or any power. I contend only with Satan
for souls and I have come to break the chains of
Satan with the fire of My love. I have come to teach
mercy, sacrifice, humility, continence. I say to you
and to everybody: "Do not crave for human wealth,
but work for eternal coins." You are deceiving
yourself if you think I am to triumph over Rome
and the ruling classes. Herods and Caesars can
sleep tranquilly, while I speak to the crowds. I have
not come to snatch anybody's sceptre... and My
eternal sceptre is already ready, but no one, unless
one was love as I am, would like to hold it. Go,
Judas, and ponder... '

'Are You rejecting me, Master?'

'I reject nobody, because who rejects does not love.
But, tell Me, Judas: how would you describe the
gesture of a man, who, knowing he is infected by a
contagious disease, says to another man who
approaches him unaware of the situation, to drink
out of his chalice: "Watch what you are doing"?
Would you define it hatred or love?'

'I would say it was love, because he does not want
the man, unaware of the danger, to ruin his
health.'

'Well, define also My gesture likewise.'

'Can I ruin my health coming with You? No, never.'

'You can ruin more than your health, because, consider this carefully, Judas, little will be debited to him who is a murderer, but believes he is doing justice, and he believes it because he does not know the Truth; but a great deal will be debited to him, who knowing the Truth, not only does not follow it, but becomes its enemy.'

'I will not do that. Take me, Master. You cannot refuse me. If You are the Saviour and You see that I am a sinner, a sheep astray, a blind man off the right path, why do You refuse to save me? Take me. I will follow You, even to death... '

'To death! That is true. Then...'

'Then, Master?'

'The future is in God's bosom. Go. We will meet tomorrow at the Fish Gate.'

'Thank You, Master. The Lord be with You.'

'And may His mercy save you.'

Jesus Works The Miracle Of The Broken Blades At The Fish Gate.

It is early morning, the sun has just risen, a beautiful clear summer day. Jesus, alone, is walking along a shady road in a little valley between two small hills-more like embankments. The hill on the left hand side is mostly covered with olive trees whereas the other hill is more barren with low mastics, thorny acacia and agave bushes. In this early morning hour, the place is deserted and with the exception of the warbling of the birds in the olive trees and the plaintive cooing of wild doves nesting in the crevices of the barren hill, there is complete peace. Even the rivulet that flows along the centre of the riverbed flows silently, gently reflecting in its depth, the green of surrounding hills that gives it its dark emerald shade.

He walks across a primitive little bridge made from a half planed tree trunk thrown across the torrent, without parapet or any protection, and continues on His way on the other bank.

In the distance, walls and gates emerge and also merchants with vegetables and foodstuffs crowding near the gates, still closed, waiting to go into town. There are donkeys braying and brawling whilst their owners scuffle in robust style. Insults and blows with cudgels are aimed at and given on donkeys' backs and human heads.

Two men are quarrelling in earnest, because the donkey of one of them has helped itself rather generously from the beautiful basket of lettuce of the other donkey and has eaten quite a lot of it! Perhaps it is only a pretext to give vent to old ill-feelings but from beneath their tunics, which reach down to their calves, they pull out two short large knives, as broad as a hand: short pointed daggers that glint in the sun. The screams of women and the shouts of men fill the air but no one tries to separate the men who are ready for a rustic duel.

Jesus, Who was walking, thoughtful, raises His head, He sees the fight and rushes between the two:

'Stop, in the name of God! 'He orders.

'No, I want to fix this cursed dog once and for all! '

'And so do I! You are fond of fringes? I'll make a fringe for you with yours bowels! '

The two move fast round Jesus, pushing Him, insulting Him to get rid of Him, trying to strike each other but without success, because Jesus, moving His mantle carefully, wards off the blows and interferes with their aiming. He gets His mantle torn.

People shout: 'Come away, Nazarene. You'll be the loser '. But He does not move and tries to calm them, reminding them of God, in vain, because the two rivals are mad with rage!

The power of miracle can be seen radiating from Jesus. For the last time He shouts: 'I order you to stop it! '

'No! Get out of the way. Go your way, dog of a Nazarene! '

Jesus then stretches out His hands, with His powerful bright look. He does not say one word. But the blades fall in pieces to the ground, as if they were made of glass, and had clashed against a rock.

The two men look at the short, useless handles, left in their hands. Astonishment deadens wrath. The astonished crowd shouts.

'And now? 'Asks Jesus, severely. 'Where is your strength? '

Also, the soldiers at the gate, attracted by the latest shouts, rush to the scene and stare, surprised and one bends down to pick up the fragments of the blades and test them on his nails, not believing they are made of steel.

'And now? 'Repeats Jesus. 'Where is your
strength? On what did you base your right? On
those bits of metal now lying in the dust? On those

splinters of metal which had no other strength but
to induce you to a sin of wrath against a brother,
thus depriving you of all the blessings of God and
consequently of all strength? Oh! How miserable
are those who rely on human means to win, and
who do not realize that holiness and not violence
will make us winners both on the earth and
beyond it! Because God is with the just.

Listen, people of Israel, and you, soldiers of Rome.
The Word of God speaks to all the sons of man,
and the Son of man will not reject the Gentiles.
The second commandment of the Lord is a
commandment of love for our neighbours. God is
good and wants good will in His children. Who is
not kindly disposed towards his neighbour, cannot
consider himself a son of God neither can he have
God in himself. Man is not an animal without
reason that rushes at and bites a prey.

Man has reason and a soul. With his reason he
must behave as a man. With his soul he must
behave as a saint. Who behaves differently, lowers
himself below animals; he stoops down to embrace
demons because a soul becomes wicked with the
sin of wrath.

Love. I say nothing else. Love your neighbour as
the Lord God of Israel prescribes. Do not always be
of Cain's blood. And why are you so? For the sake
of a few coins, you who might have become
murderers. For a few palms of land. For a better
position. For a woman. What are such things? Are
they eternal? No. They last less than a lifetime,
which lasts an instant of eternity. And what do you
lose if you follow them? The eternal peace
promised to the just, and which the Messiah will
bring you together with in His Kingdom. Come on

to the way of Truth. Follow the Voice of God. Love one another. Be honest. Be moderate. Be humble and fair. Go and meditate. '

'Who are You who speak such words and break swords with Your will power? Only One can do such things: the Messiah. Not even John the Baptist is greater than He is. Are You perhaps the Messiah? 'Three or four people ask Him.

'Yes, I am. '

'You? Are You the One who cures sick people and preaches God in Galilee? '

'I am. '

'I have an old mother who is dying. Cure her! '

'And I, see? I am losing all my strength because of my pains. My children are still young. Cure me! '

'Go home. Your mother this evening will prepare your supper; and you: be healed. I want it! 'The crowd roars with joy. They then ask: 'Your Name! Your Name! '

'Jesus of Nazareth. '

'Jesus! Jesus! Hosanna! Hosanna! '

The crowd is jubilant. The donkeys can now do what they like; no one pays attention to them. Mothers rush out from the town as the news has quickly spread and they lift up their little ones. Jesus blesses and smiles. And He tries to make His way through the acclaiming crowd to enter into the town and continue on His way but the crowd will not hear of it. 'Stay with us! In Judaea! In Judaea! We are the sons of Abraham, too! 'They shout.

'Master! 'Judas runs towards Him. 'Master, You arrived before me. But what is happening? '

'The Rabbi has worked a miracle! Not in Galilee; here! We want Him here! '

'See, Master? The whole of Israel loves You. It is only fair You should stay here, too. Why do You not want to? '

'It is not that I do not want to, Judas. I came here by Myself, that the roughness of the Galilean disciples might not irritate the subtleness of the Judaeans. I want to gather all the sheep of Israel under the sceptre of God. '

'That is why I said to You: "Take me". I am a Judaean, and I know how to deal with my equals. Will You therefore remain in Jerusalem? '

'For a few days. To wait for a disciple, who is also a Judaean. Then I will go through Judaea... '

'Oh! I will come with You. I will accompany You. You will come to my village. I will take You to my house. Will You come, Master? '

'I will come... Have you any news of the Baptist, since you are a Judaean and you live with the mighty ones? '

'I know that he is still in jail, but they want to set him free, because the crowds are threatening a revolt, if they do not get their prophet. Do You know him? '

'Yes, I do. '

'Do You like, him? What do You think of him? '

'I think no one has been more like Elijah than he is. '

'Do You really consider him the Precursor? '

'Yes, he is. He is the morning star announcing the sun. Blessed are those who through his preaching have prepared themselves for the Sun. '

'John is very severe. '

'Not more with others than he is with himself. '

'That is true. But it is difficult to follow him in his penance. You are more kind, and it is easy to love You. '

'And yet... '

'Yet... what, Master? '

'Yet, as he is hated because of his austerity, I will be hated because of My goodness, because they both preach God, and God is disliked by the wicked. But it is to be thus. As he precedes Me in preaching, so he will precede Me in death. Woe to the killers of Penance- and Goodness. '

'Why, Master, have You always such sad forecasts? The crowds love You. You saw that... '

'Because I am sure. Humble people do love Me. But the crowd is not all humble and of humble people. But I am not sad. It is a Placid vision of the future and compliance with the will of the Father, Who sent Me for that. And I have come for that. Here we are at the Temple. I am going to the Bel Midrash** to teach the crowds. If you wish, you may stay. '

'I will stay with You. There in only one thing I wish: to serve You and let You triumph. '

**Bel Midrash is the part of the Temple where doctors used to teach people.

Jesus Preaches In The Temple. Judas Iscariot Is With Him.

Jesus walks into the Temple enclosure with Judas by His side. They cross the first terrace and stop in a porch alongside a wide yard paved with multi-coloured marble. The yard is beautiful and crowded.

Jesus looks round for a spot, sees one He likes but before heading for it, He says to Judas: ' Call the official of the place for Me. I must make Myself known, so that no one may say I break the custom and lack in respect. '

'Master, You are above the custom, and no one more than You is entitled to speak in the House of God, since You are His Messiah. '

'I know, you know, but they do not know. I have not come to scandalize or to teach people to break, not only the Law, but also the custom. On the contrary, I have come to teach respect, humility and obedience and to remove scandals. I therefore want to ask to be allowed to speak in God's name, making the official of the place acknowledge Me as being worthy. '

'You did not do that the last time. '

'The last time I was inflamed by the zeal for the House of God, desecrated by too many things. The last time I was the Son of the Father, the Heir Who in the name of the Father and for the love of My House, acted in His majesty, which is above officials and priests. Now I am the Master of Israel, and I teach Israel also that. After all, Judas, do you think that a disciple is greater than His Master? '

'No, Jesus. '

'And who are you? And who am I? '

'You are the Master, I the disciple. '

'Well then, if you admit that, why do you want to teach your Master? Go and obey. I obey My Father, you must obey your Master. The first condition of the Son of God: to obey without discussing orders, knowing that the Father can give but holy orders. The first condition of a disciple: to obey his Master, knowing that the Master knows, and can give but just orders.'

'It is true. Forgive me. I will obey. '

'I forgive you. Go. And, Judas, listen to one more thing: remember that. Always bear that in mind in future. '

'To obey? Yes, I will. '

'No: remember that I was respectful and humble to the Temple. To the Temple: that is, to the mighty castes; go.' Judas looks at Him, wistfully and inquisitively... but he dares not ask any more questions and he goes away thoughtfully.

... He comes back with a sumptuously dressed personage. 'Here, Master, the official. '

'Peace be with you. I ask to teach Israel, amongst the rabbis of Israel.'

'Are You a rabbi? '

'Yes, I am. '

'Who was Your teacher? '

'The Spirit of God Who speaks to Me in His wisdom and enlightens for Me every word of the Holy Scriptures.'

'Are You greater than Hillel, since You say You know all doctrines, without a teacher? How can one be formed if there is no one forming him? '

'As David was formed, an unknown little shepherd,
who became a powerful and wise king by God's
will. '

'Your Name? '

'Jesus of Joseph of Jacob, of the House of David,
and of Mary of Joachim of the House of David, and
of Anne of Aaron, Mary, the Virgin married in the

Temple by the High Priest, according to the law of Israel, because She was an orphan.'

'Who can prove that? '

'There must still be some Levites here who will remember the event and who were the same age as Zacharias of the class of Abijah, My relative. Ask them, if you doubt My sincerity. '

'I believe You. But who will prove to me that You are capable of teaching? '

'Listen to Me and you will judge yourself. '

'You are free to do it... But... are You not a Nazarene? '

'I was born at Bethlehem of Judah, at the time of the census decreed by Caesar. Banished by unfair orders, the children of David are now everywhere. But the family is of Judah. '

'You know... the Pharisees... all Judaea... throughout Galilee... '

'I know. But be reassured. I was born at Bethlehem, at Bethlehem Ephrathah, whence My family comes; if now I live in Galilee, it is only to fulfil the given sign... '

The official goes away a few yards, hastening to where they call him. Judas asks: 'Why did You not say that You are the Messiah? '

'My words will say so. '

'Which is the sign to be fulfilled? '

'The union of Israel under the teaching of the word of Christ. I am the Shepherd of Whom the Prophets speak and I have come to gather all the sheep of every region, I have come to cure the sick ones, and put the wandering ones on a good pasture. There is no Judaea or Galilee, no Decapolis or Idumaea for Me. There is only one thing: the Love that sees with one glance only and joins in one embrace only in order to save... 'Jesus is inspired. Rays of light seem to be emanating from Him, so happily He smiles at his dream. Judas, amazed, stares at Him.

Some curious people come closer to them, drawn, fascinated and struck by the difference in their magnificence. Jesus lowers His head and smiles at the little group with a smile, the sweetness of which no painter will ever be able to portray and no believer, who has never seen it, will ever be able to imagine. And He says: 'Come if you are anxious to hear eternal words. '

He goes towards the arch of the porch, and leaning against a column, begins to speak, using that morning's event as a starting point.

'This morning, on entering Zion, I saw two children of Abraham who were ready to kill each other for a few coins. I could have cursed them in the name of God, because God says: "You shall not kill" and He also says that who does not maintain the Law is to be cursed. But I felt pity for their ignorance of the spirit of the Law and I only prevented them from committing murder, that they may have the opportunity of repenting, knowing God, serving Him in obedience, loving not only those who love them, but also their enemies.

Yes, Israel. A new day is dawning for you and the commandment of love is becoming brighter. Does the year begin with the foggy Ethanim, or with the sad Chislev, the days of which are shorter than a dream and the nights longer than a calamity? No, it begins with the flowery, sunny, happy Nisan, when everything smiles and the heart of man, even the poorest and saddest one, opens up to hope, because summer is coming, with its crops, sunshine and fruit, when it is sweet to sleep on a meadow full of flowers, under a starry sky, and it is easy for man to nourish himself, because every clod of earth bears herbs or fruit to satisfy his hunger.

Here, Israel. Winter, the time of expectation, is over. Here is now the joy of the promise which is being accomplished. The Bread and Wine are about to be poured out to satisfy your hunger and your thirst. The Sun is among you. Everything breathes more freely and tastes sweeter under this Sun. Also the precept of our Law: the first and most holy of the holy precepts: "Love your God and love your neighbour".

In the dim light granted to you so far, you were told: "Love those who love you and hate your enemies": you could not have done any better, because the wrath of God still weighed upon you, owing to Adam's sin of estrangement. And your enemy was not only who crossed the borders of your fatherland, but also who did you wrong privately or you thought he had done. Hatred, therefore, was smouldering in every heart, because which man, intentionally or unintentionally, does not give offence to his brother? And which man reaches an old age without being offended?

I say to you: love also those who offend you. Do that, considering that Adam, and every man through him, is a sinner against God, and there is no one who can say: "I have not offended God". And yet, God forgives, not once only He forgives, but dozens of times, He forgives thousands of times, as it is proved by the fact that man still exists on the earth. Forgive therefore, as God forgives.

And if you cannot do it out of love for the brother who injured you, do it for the love of God, Who gives you bread and life, Who protects you in your worldly needs, and has arranged all events to procure eternal peace for you in His bosom. This is the new law, the law of God's springtime, of the flowery time of Grace amongst men, of the time that will bear you a matchless Fruit that will open the gates of Heaven for you.

The voice that spoke in the desert is no longer heard. But it is not mute. It still speaks to God on behalf of Israel and still speaks to every Israelite with an honest heart and it says: "The Lamb of God, He Who takes away the sins of the world, Who will baptize with the fire of the Holy Spirit is amongst you. He will clear His threshing-floor and gather His wheat."

– after teaching you to do penance to prepare the ways to the Lord Who is coming, and to be charitable giving what is surplus to those who lack even what is necessary, and to be honest without extorting and vexing.

Endeavour to recognize Him Whom the Precursor indicates to you. His suffering is imploring God to give you light. See. May your spiritual eyes be opened. You will recognize the Light that is coming. I pick up the voice of the Prophet announcing the Messiah, and with the power I receive from the Father, I amplify it and I add My authority to it and I call you to the truth of the Law. Prepare your hearts for the grace of the oncoming Redemption. The Redeemer is amongst you. Blessed are those who will be worthy of being redeemed, because they are men of good will. Peace be with you. '

Someone asks: 'Are You a disciple of the Baptist, since You speak of him with such veneration? '

'I was baptized by him, on the banks of the Jordan, before he was imprisoned. I venerate him because he is holy in the eyes of God. I solemnly tell you that among the children of Abraham there is no one greater in grace than he is. From his birth to his death, the eyes of God will rest upon that blessed man without any feeling of disdain. '

'Did he give You any assurance about the Messiah? '

'His word, which does not lie, pointed out the living Messiah to those present.'

'Where? When? '

'When it was time to do so. '

But Judas feels bound to say to everybody: 'The Messiah is He Who is speaking to you. I declare it, because I know Him, and I am His first disciple. '

'Him!... Oh!... 'The people move away frightened. But Jesus is so sweet that they gather round Him again.

'Ask Him to work some miracles. He is powerful. He can cure. He can read your hearts. He can answer all your questions. '

'Tell Him, on my behalf, that I am not well. My right eye is blind. My left one is already failing... '

'Master. '

Jesus, Who is caressing a little girl, turns round.

'Master, this man is almost blind and he wants to see. I told him you can... '

'I can cure who has faith. Have you faith, man? '

'I believe in the God of Israel. I come here to enter the Bethzatha Pool. But there is always someone before me. '

'Can you believe in Me? '

'If I believe in the angel of the pool, should I not believe in You, Who Your disciple says is the Messiah? '

Jesus smiles. He wets His finger with saliva and lightly touches the diseased eye. 'What can you see? '

'I see things without the fog I used to see. Are You not curing the other one? '

Jesus smiles once again. He repeats the operation on the blind eye. 'What can you see? 'He asks, removing His fingertip from the closed eyelid.

'Ah! Lord of Israel! I can see as well as when I was a little boy, running on the meadows! May You be blessed forever and ever! 'The man cries, kneeling at Jesus' feet.

'Go. Be good, now, out of gratitude to God. '

A Levite who arrived towards the end of the miracle, asks: 'On what authority do You do such things? '

'Are you asking Me? I will tell you, if you answer a question. According to you, who is greater, a prophet who prophesies the Messiah or the Messiah Himself? '

'What a question! The Messiah is greater: He is the Redeemer promised by the Most High! '

'Well, then, why did the Prophets work miracles? On what authority? '

'On the authority given to them by God to prove to the crowds that God was with them. '

'Well, I work miracles on the same authority: God is with Me, I am with Him. And I thus prove to the people that what I say is true and that the Messiah, with a greater right and a greater power, can do what the Prophets were able to do. '

The Levite goes away thoughtful.

Jesus Teaches Judas Iscariot.

Jesus and Judas have just finished praying in the Temple, in the area closest to the Holy of Holies, where the Jewish males pray.

Judas would like to remain with Jesus but the Master objects: 'Judas, I want to be alone at night time. At night, My spirit gets its nourishment from the Father. Prayer, meditation and solitude are more necessary for Me than material food. Who wishes to live for the spirit, and lead others to live the same life, must disregard the flesh, nay, I would say: kill it, to devote all his attention to the spirit. Everybody must do that, you know Judas. You, too, if you really want to belong to God, that is to the supernatural. '

'But we are still on the earth, Master. How can we neglect the flesh and take care only of the spirit? Is what You say not the antithesis of God's commandment: "You shall not kill"? Does the commandment not forbid also suicide? If life is a gift from God, must we love it, or not? '

'I will not reply to you as I would reply to a simple-minded man, for whom it is enough to raise his soul or his mind to supernatural spheres, so that we can take him with us flying in spiritual kingdoms. You are not a simple-minded person. You were formed in an environment that refined you... and it also marred you with its quibbles and doctrines. Do you remember Solomon, Judas? He was wise, the wisest man of those times. Do you remember what he said, after acquiring all knowledge? "Vanity of vanities, all is vanity. To fear God and observe His commandments, that is all that matters to man." Now I tell you that it is necessary to know how to get nourishment, but no poison, from food. And if we know that a food is bad for us, because it is not wholesome and therefore causes harm in us, we must take no more of that food, even if it is pleasant to our taste. Plain bread and water from the fountain are better than the sophisticated dishes of the king's table, containing drugs which upset and poison. '

'What must I leave, Master? '

'Everything you know that upsets you. Because God is peace and if you want to follow the path of God, you must clear your mind, your heart and your flesh of everything that is not peace giving and causes anxiety. I know it is difficult to amend one's way of living. But I am here to help you. I am here to help man to become the son of God once again, to re-create himself by means of a new creation, of an autogenesis wanted by man himself. But let Me reply to your question, so that you may not say that you were left in error through a fault of Mine. It is true that to kill oneself is the same as killing other people. Both our own and other people's lives are the gift of God and only God Who gives life, has the authority to take it. Who kills himself, confesses his own pride, and pride is hated by God. '

'He confesses his pride? I would say his despair. '

'And what is despair but pride? Just think, Judas. Why does one despair? Either because misfortunes continuously upset him and he wants to overcome them by himself, but is unable to do so. Or because he is guilty and he thinks that he cannot be forgiven by God. In both cases, is not pride the basic reason? The man who wants to do all by himself, is no longer humble enough to stretch out his hand to the Father and say to Him: "I am not able, but You are. Help me, because I hope and wait for everything from You." The other man who says: "God cannot forgive me" says so, because measuring God by his own standards, he knows that another person could not forgive him, if that person had been offended, as he offended God. So here again it is pride. A humble man understands and forgives, even if he suffers for the offence received. A proud man does not forgive. He is proud also because he is not capable of lowering his head and saying: "Father, I have sinned, forgive Your poor guilty son." But do you not know, Judas, that the Father will forgive everything, if one asks to be forgiven with a sincere, contrite, humble, heart willing to rise again to new life?'

'But certain crimes are not to be forgiven. They cannot be forgiven. '

'That is what you say. And it will be true only because man wants it to be true. But, oh! I solemnly tell you that even after the crime of crimes, if the guilty man should rush to the Father's feet – He is called Father, Judas, just for that, and He is a Father of infinite perfection – and crying, implored Him to be forgiven, offering to expiate, without despairing, the Father would make it possible for him to expiate and thus deserve forgiveness and save his soul. '

'Well, then, You say that the men quoted by the Scriptures who killed themselves, did wrong. '

'It is not lawful to do violence to anybody, not even to oneself. They did wrong. In their limited knowledge of good, perhaps in certain cases, they had mercy from God. But after the Word has clarified the truth and has given strength to spirits with His Spirit, then who dies in despair will no longer be forgiven. Neither in the instant of the personal judgement, nor after centuries of Gehenna, on Doomsday, never! Is that hardness on God's side? No: it is justice. God will say: "You, a creature gifted with reason and supernatural knowledge, created free by Me, you decided to follow the path you chose and you said: 'God will not forgive me. I am separated from Him forever. I think I must apply the law by myself to my own crime. I am parting from life to evade remorse' without considering that you would no longer have felt remorse if you had come on My faithful bosom. And let it be done to you, as you judged. I will not do violence to the freedom I gave you." That is what the Eternal Father will say to the suicide. Meditate on it, Judas. Life is a gift, a gift to be loved. But what gift is it? A holy gift. So love it holily. Life lasts as long as the flesh holds out. Then the great Life, the eternal Life begins. A Life of blissful happiness for the just, of malediction for the unjust. Is life a purpose or a means? It is a means. It serves for a purpose which is eternity. Then let us give life what is required to make it last and serve the spirit in its conquest. The exercise of self-restraint of the flesh in all its lusts, in all of them. Self-restraint of the mind in all its desires, in all of them. Self-restraint of the heart in all human passions. Infinite instead is to be the ardour for heavenly passions: love of God and the neighbour, obedience to the divine word, heroism in good and virtue. I have given you the answer, Judas. Are you convinced? Is the explanation satisfactory? Be always sincere, and ask when you do not yet know enough: I am here to be your Master. '

'I have understood and it is satisfactory. But...it is very difficult to do what I have understood. You can... because You are holy. But... I am a man, young and full of life... '

'I have come for men, Judas. Not for the angels. They do not need a teacher. They see God. They live in His Paradise. They are not unaware of the passions of men, because the Intelligence which is their Life makes them acquainted with everything, also those who are not guardians of men. But, spiritual as they are, they can have but one sin, as one of them had, and he drew to his side those who were weaker in charity: pride, the arrow that disfigured Lucifer, the most beautiful of the archangels, and turned him into the horrifying monster of the Abyss. I have not come for the angels, who, after Lucifer's fall, are horrified even at the shadow of a proud thought. But I have come for men. To make angels of men. Man was the perfection of creation. He had the spirit of the angel and the full beauty of the animal, complete in all its animal and moral parts. There was no creature equal to him. He was the king of the earth, as God is the King of Heaven, and one day, when he would have fallen asleep for the last time on the earth, he would have become king with the Father in Heaven. Satan tore the wings off the angel-man and he replaced them with the claws of a beast and with intense yearning for filth, and lured him into becoming a being which is better described as a man-demon, rather than simply a man. I want to eradicate the disfigurement worked by Satan, as well as the corrupted craving of the contaminated flesh. I want to give back to man his wings, and make him once again king, coheir of the Father and of the Celestial Kingdom. I know that man, if he is willing, can do what I say, to become once again king and angel. I would not tell you things you could not do. I am not one of the rhetors** who preach impossible doctrines. I have real flesh, so that through the experience of the flesh, I might learn which are the temptations of man. '

** A teacher of rhetoric in ancient Greece and Rome

'And what about sins? '

'Everyone can be tempted. Sinners are only those who want to be such. '

'Have You ever sinned, Jesus? '

'No, I never wanted to sin. Not because I am the Son of the Father. But because I wanted and I want to prove to man that the Son of man did not sin because He did not want to sin, and that man can, if he wants, not sin. '

'Have You ever been tempted? '

'I am thirty years old, Judas. And I did not live in a cave upon a mountain. I lived amongst men. And if I had been in the loneliest place in the world, do you think temptations would not have come to Me? We have everything in us: good and evil[1]. We carry everything with us. And the breath of God blows on the good and enlivens it like a thurible*** of sweet-smelling holy incense. And Satan blows on evil, thus kindling a furious blazing fire. But diligent good will and constant prayer are like damp sand on the hellish fire: they suffocate it and put it out. '

*** A **thurible** is a metal censer suspended from chains, in which incense is burned during worship services.

'But if You have never sinned, how can You judge sinners? '

'I am a man and the Son of God. What I might ignore as a man and judge wrongly, I know and judge as the Son of God. After all!... Judas, answer this question of Mine. Will one who is hungry, suffer more by saying: "I will now sit down at the table" or by saying: "There is no food for me"? '

'He suffers more if there is no food, because the simple thought that he is without food, will bring back to him the pleasant smell of food and his bowels will be tortured by biting desire. '

'Right: temptation is as biting as that desire, Judas. Satan makes it more intense, more real, more alluring than any accomplished act. Further, the act satisfies, and at times nauseates; whereas temptations do not subside, but like pruned trees, they grow stronger and stronger. '

'And have You never yielded? '

'No, never. '

'How did You manage? '

'I said: "Father, lead Me not into temptation." '

'What? You, the Messiah, You work miracles and You ask Your Father for help? '

'Not only for help: I ask Him not to lead Me into temptation. Do you think that I, simply because of Who I am, can do without the Father? Oh! no! I solemnly tell you that the Father grants everything to His Son, and that the Son receives everything from the Father. And I tell you that everything the Father will be asked for in My name will be granted. But here we are at Gethsemane, where I live. You can see the first trees beyond the walls. You live beyond Tophet. It is getting dark already. You had better not come up as far as that. We will meet again tomorrow at the same place. Goodbye. Peace be with you. '

'Peace be with You, too, Master... But I would like to tell You another thing. I will come with You as far as the Kidron, then I will come back. Why do You live in such a humble place? You know, people notice so many things. Do You not know anyone in town with a beautiful house? If You wish, I can take You to some friends. They will give You hospitality because of my friendly attitude towards them; and the house would be more worthy of You. '

'Do you think so? I do not. All classes of people are worthy or unworthy. And without lacking in charity, but to avoid offending justice, I tell you that the unworthy, the mischievously unworthy, are often to be found amongst the great ones. It is not necessary and it is of no use being influential, to be good or to hide sins from the eyes of God. Everything will be turned over under My Sign. And not who is mighty will be great, but who is humble and holy. '

'But to be respected, to impose oneself... '

'Is Herod respected? Is Caesar respected? No, they are endured and cursed both by lips and by hearts. And believe Me, Judas, on good people, or simply on people of good will, it will be easier for Me to impose Myself with modesty rather than with majesty. '

'But... will You always despise the mighty ones? You will make enemies of them! I was thinking of speaking of You to many people I know and who are influential... '

'I will not despise anybody. I will meet the poor as well as the rich, slaves as well as kings, pure people as well as sinners. But if I have to be grateful to those who provide Me with bread and a roof that I may carry on My work, whatever the roof and the bread may be, I will always give My preference to the humble. The great ones already have so many joys. The poor have but their honest conscience, a faithful love, children and the joy of being listened to by those who are above them. I will always be bent over the poor, the afflicted, and sinners. I thank you for your good intention. But leave Me to this place of peace and prayer. Go, and may God inspire you with what is good. '

And Jesus leaves the disciple and goes into the olive-grove.

Jesus Meets John of Zebedee at Gethsemane.

When Jesus draws nearer to the little low white house in the middle of the olive- grove, a young man carrying pruning and hoeing tools in his hand, greets Him.

'God be with You, Rabbi: 'Your disciple John came and he just left to come and meet You.

'How long ago? '

'Not long, he has just passed that path. We thought You were coming from Bethany... '

Jesus starts walking very fast, He goes round the cliff, He sees John walking at a near running pace down towards the town and calls him. John turns round, his face brightened with joy and he shouts: 'Oh! My Master! 'And he starts running back.

Jesus receives him with His arms wide open and they embrace each other affectionately.

'I was coming to look for You... We thought You had been to Bethany, as You told us. '

'Yes, I wanted to go. I must start evangelising also the surroundings of Jerusalem. But I stayed in town... to teach a new disciple. '

'Everything You do is well done, Master. And is always successful. See? Even now we met very soon. '

They begin walking, and Jesus places an arm on John's shoulders, who, being shorter, looks up at Him, obviously very happy for so much intimacy. They thus start going back to the little house.

'Have you been here long? '

'No, Master. I left Doco at dawn, together with Simon, to whom I gave Your message. Then we stopped in the country of Bethany, shared the food we had and spoke of You to the peasants we found in the fields. When it was cooler, we parted. Simon went to see a friend of his, to whom he wants to speak about You. He owns almost the whole of Bethany. He has known him for a long time, when their fathers were alive. But Simon is coming here tomorrow. He asked me to tell You that he is happy to serve You. Simon is very clever. I would like to be like him. But I am an ignorant boy. '

'No, John, you are doing very well, too. '

'Are You really satisfied with Your poor John? '

'Yes, I am thoroughly satisfied, My dear John. Thoroughly satisfied. '

'Oh! My Master! 'John bends down with eagerness to take Jesus, hand, which he kisses and passes lovingly over his face, as if caressing it.

They have arrived at the little house. They enter the low smoky kitchen and the landlord greets them:

'Peace be with You. '

'Peace to this house, to you and to those who live here with you. I have a disciple with Me. '

'There will be bread and oil for him, too. '

'I brought some dried fish that James and Peter gave me. And passing by Nazareth, Your Mother gave me some bread and honey for You. I walked all the time without stopping, but it will be dry now. '

'It does not matter, John. It will always have the flavour of My Mother's hands.'

John pulls out his treasures from the knapsack that he had put in a corner. They steep the dried fish for a few minutes in hot water, then they put some olive oil on it and then they roast it on the fire.

Jesus blesses the food and sits at the table with His disciple, the landlord, Jonah, and Jonah's son. The landlady comes and goes bringing fish, some black olives, boiled vegetables dressed with oil. Jesus offers also some honey. And He offers it also to the landlady, spreading it on some bread. 'It comes from My beehive 'He says. 'My Mother looks after the bees. Eat it. It is good...' but Mary does not want to deprive Him of the sweet honey so He adds '...You are so good to Me, Mary, and you deserve much more than this '

Supper only lasts a short while during which they converse on common topics. Once super is finished, they give thanks for the food and then Jesus says to John: 'Come. Let us go out into the olive-grove for a little while. It is a clear, mild night. It will be pleasant to be out there for a short time. '

'Master, I say "good night" to You...' Says Jonah '... I am tired and also my son is tired. We are going to bed. I will leave the door ajar and the lamp on the table. You know what to do. '

'Go, Jonah. And put out the lamp. There is such a bright moonlight, that we will be able to see without any light. '

'But where will Your disciple sleep? '

'With Me. On My mat there is room also for him. Is that right, John? 'John is enraptured at the idea of sleeping beside Jesus.

Before they depart, John takes something out of the knapsack in the corner and then they go out into the olive-grove where they walk for a little while until they reach a brow which commands a view of the whole of Jerusalem.

'Let us sit down here and talk a little 'says Jesus.

But John prefers to sit at Jesus' feet on the short grass, and he rests his arm on Jesus' knees, with his head reclined on his arm, looking now and again at Jesus. He looks like a little boy near the person dearest to him. 'It is beautiful also here, Master. Look how large the town seems at night. Larger than by day. '

'It is because the moonlight shades the outlines. See: the borders seem to widen out in a silver brightness. Look at the top of the Temple, up there. Does it not look as if it were suspended in mid-air. '

'It seems supported by angels on their silver wings. 'Jesus sighs.

'Why are You sighing, Master? '

'Because the angels have abandoned the Temple. Its feature of purity and holiness is now confined to its walls only. Those who should impress it into its soul – because every place has its soul, that is the spirit for which it was built, and the Temple has, or should have, a soul of prayer and holiness – those who should energize such spirit, are instead the first to suffocate it. You cannot give what you do not possess, John. And if there are many priests and Levites living there, not even one tenth of them are capable of giving life to the Holy Place. They give death instead. They transmit the death of their own souls, which are dead to what is holy. They have their formulae. But they do not have the essence of them. They are corpses that are warm only because putrefaction swells them. '

'Have they done You wrong, Master? 'John is all upset.

'No. On the contrary they allowed Me to speak when I asked to. '

'Did You ask them? Why? '

'Because I do not want to be the one who starts war. There will be war in any case. Because I will be the cause of a silly human fear for some, and the cause of reproach for others. But this must be written in their book, not in Mine. '

They sit in silence for a few moments.

'Master, I know Annas and Caiaphas. My family
has been on business relations with them, and
when I came to Judaea to see John, I used to come
to the Temple, and they were good to the son of
Zebedee. My father always sends them the best
fish.

That is the custom, You know? If you want them to
be friendly and to continue so, you must do that...'

'I know. ' Jesus is serious.

'Well, if You wish, I will speak to the High Priest
about You. And... if You want, I know a man who
is on business terms with my father. He is a rich
fish merchant. He has a lovely big house near the
Hippicus Tower, because they are very rich people,
but they are also very good. You would be more
comfortable and You would not get so tired. To
come here, You have to come through the suburb
of Ophel, which is so wild and always full of
donkeys and quarrelsome boys. '

'No, John. Thank you. But I am all right here. See
how much peace there is? I told also the other
disciple who made the same suggestion. He said:
"To enjoy a higher reputation." '

'I mentioned it that You might not get so tired. '

'I do not get tired. I will walk so much, and I will
never tire. Do you know what tires Me?
Indifference. Oh! What a burden it is! It is like
carrying a weight on your heart. '

'I love You, Jesus. '

'Yes, and you comfort Me. I love you so much, John, and I always will, because you will never betray Me. '

'Betray You! Oh! '

'And yet there will be many who will betray Me... John, listen. I told you that I stayed here to teach a new disciple. He is a young Jew, educated and well known. '

'Well, then. You will have to work much less with him than You have to with us, Master. I am glad that You have someone who is more capable than we are.'

'Do you think I will work less? '

'Yes, if he is less ignorant than we are, he will understand You better, and serve You better, especially if he loves You. '

'What you say is right. But love is not proportionate to education or formation. A virgin loves with all the strength of her first love. That applies also to the virginity of mind. And the beloved penetrates and is more deeply impressed on a virgin heart and a virgin mind, rather than on hearts and minds imbued with other loves. But if God wants... Listen, John. I would ask you to be friendly with him. My heart shudders at the thought of putting you, an unshorn lamb, near the expert in life. But it subsides considering that you may well be a lamb, but you are also an eagle, and if the expert tries to make you touch the muddy ground, the soil of good human sense, with a stroke of your wings, you will be able to free yourself and desire only the clear blue sky and the sun. That is why I ask you to remain as you are and be friendly to the new disciple, inspiring him with your love, because he will not be loved very much by Simon Peter and the others...'

'Oh! Master! Are You not sufficient? '

'I am the Master. Not everything will be said to Me. You are a companion, a little younger, to whom it will be easier for him to unbosom himself. I am not suggesting you should repeat to Me what he tells you. I detest spies and traitors. But I ask you to evangelize him with your faith, your charity, your purity, John. It is a land defiled by stagnant waters. It must be dried up by the sun of love, purified by the integrity of thoughts, desires and deeds, and cultivated with faith. You can do that. '

'If You say I can... Yes! If You say I can do that, I will do it. For Your sake...'

'Thank you, John. '

'Master, You mentioned Simon Peter. And that reminded me of something I should have told You immediately, but the joy of listening to You made me forget about it. When we went back to Capernaum after Pentecost, we found the usual amount of money from that unknown person. The boy had taken it to my mother. I gave it to Peter, and he handed it back to me, saying I should use some of it on my way back and on my stay at Doco and then bring You the rest, for whatever need of Yours... because also Peter thought this place might not be comfortable... but You say it is... I took only two coins for two poor people I met near Ephraim. For the rest, I lived with what my mother had given me and what I was given by some good people to whom I preached Your Name. Here is the purse. '

'We will give the money to the poor tomorrow. So Judas also will be acquainted with our custom. '

'Has Your cousin come? How was he so quick? He was at Nazareth and he did not tell me he was leaving... '

'No. Judas is the new disciple. He comes from Kerioth. But you saw him at Passover, here, the evening I cured Simon. He was with Thomas. '

'Ah! It's him? 'John is a little perplexed.

'Yes, it is he. And what is Thomas doing? '

'He carried out Your instructions, he left Simon the Cananean and went by the sea road to meet Philip and Bartholomew. '

'Yes, I want you to love one another, without preferences, helping one another mutually and bearing with one another. No one is perfect, John. Neither the young nor the old. But if you have a good will, you will reach perfection and what is wanting in you, I will supply. You are like the children of a holy family. In it there are very different characters. One is strong, another is sweet, or brave, or shy, or impulsive or very cautious. If you were all alike, you would be really strong in one character, but very weak in all the others. Whereas you thus form a perfect union, completed by you all. Love unites you, it must unite you, for the sake of God's cause. '

'And for Your sake, Jesus. '

'First the cause of God and then the love for His Christ. '

'I... and what am I in our family? '

'You are the loving peace of the Christ of God. Are you tired, John? Do you want to go back? I will stay here and pray. '

'I will stay, too, and I will pray with You. Let me stay and pray with You. '

'You may stay. '

Jesus says some psalms and John prays with Him. But his voice dies down and he falls asleep with his head on Jesus' lap. Jesus smiles, covers the shoulders of the sleeping disciple with His mantle and continues to pray silently.

Jesus With Judas Iscariot Meets Simon Zealot And John.

'Are You sure he will come? 'Asks Judas Iscariot as he walks up and down with Jesus near one of the gates within the Temple enclosure.

'I am certain. He was leaving Bethany at dawn and at Gethsemane he was to meet My first disciple... '

There is a pause. Then Jesus stops in front of Judas and stares at him, studying him closely. Then He places a hand on Judas' shoulder and asks: ' Why, Judas, do you not tell Me your thoughts? '

'What thoughts? I have no special thought, Master, at the present moment. I ask You even too many questions. You certainly cannot complain of my muteness. '

'You ask Me many questions and You give Me many details on the town and its inhabitants. But you do not unburden yourself to Me. What do you think it matters to Me, what you tell Me about the wealth of people and the members of this or that family? I am not an idler who has come here to while away the time. You know why I have come. And you may well realize that I am concerned with being the Master of My disciples, as the most important thing. I therefore want sincerity and trust from them. Was your father fond of you, Judas? '

'He was very fond of me. He was proud of me. When I went back home from school, and even later, when I went back to Kerioth from Jerusalem, he wanted me to tell him everything. He took an interest in everything I did and he would rejoice if they were good things, he would comfort me if they were not so good, if sometimes, You know, we all make mistakes – if I had made a mistake and had been blamed for it, he would show me the fairness of the reproach I had received, or the injustice of my action. But he did it so gently... he seemed an older brother. He always ended by saying: "I am saying this because I want my Judas to be just. I want to be blessed through my son." My father... '

Jesus, Who has carefully observed how moved Judas is at the recall of the memories of his father, says: 'Now, Judas, be sure of what I am going to tell you. Nothing will make your father so happy, as your being a faithful disciple. Your father, who brought you up as you said, must have been a just man and his soul will rejoice, where he is awaiting the light, seeing that you are My disciple. But in order to be such, you must say to yourself: "I have found my lost father, the father who was like an older brother to me, I have found him in my Jesus, and I will tell Him everything, as I used to tell my beloved father, over whose death I am still mourning, that I may receive from Him guidance, blessings or a kind reproach." May God grant it, and above all may you behave so that Jesus will always say to you: "You are good. I bless you." '

'Oh! Yes, Jesus! If You love me so much, I will strive to be good, as You want and my father wanted me to be. And my mother will no longer have an aching pain in her heart. She used to say: "You have no guide now, my son, and you still need one so much." When she knows that I have You! '

'I will love you as no other man could possibly love you, I will love you so much, I do love you. Do not disappoint Me. '

'No, Master, I will not. I was full of conflicts. Envy, jealousy, eagerness to excel, sensuality, everything clashed in me against the voice of my conscience. Even quite recently, see? You caused me to suffer. That is: no, not You. It was my wicked nature... I thought I was Your first disciple... and, now You have just told me that You already have one. '

'You saw him yourself. Do you not remember that at Passover I was in the Temple with many Galileans? '

'I thought they were friends... I thought I was the first one to be chosen for such destiny, and that I was therefore the dearest. '

'There are no distinctions in My heart between the first and the last. If the first one should err and the last one were a holy man, then there would be a distinction in the eyes of God. But I will love just the same: I will love the holy living man with a blissful love, and the sinner with a suffering love. But here is John coming with Simon. John, My first disciple, Simon, the one of whom I spoke to you two days ago. You have already seen Simon and John. One was ill...'

'Ah! The leper! I remember. Is he already Your disciple? '

'Since the following day. '

'And why did I have to wait so long? '

'Judas?! '

'You are right. Forgive me. '

John sees the Master, points Him out to Simon and they make haste.

John and the Master kiss each other. Simon, instead, throws himself at Jesus' feet and kisses them, exclaiming: 'Glory to my Saviour! Bless Your servant that his actions may be holy in the eyes of God and that I may glorify Him and bless Him for giving You to me. '

Jesus places His hand on Simon's head: 'Yes, I bless you to thank you for your work. Get up, Simon. This is John, and this is Simon: here is My last disciple. He also wants to follow the Truth. He is therefore a brother to you all. '

They greet each other: the two Judaeans
inquisitively, John heartily.

'Are you tired, Simon? 'Asks Jesus.

'No, Master. With my health I have recovered a vitality I never felt before. '

'And I know you make good use of it. I have spoken to many people and they all told Me that you have already instructed them about the Messiah. '

Simon smiles happily. 'Also last night I spoke of You to one who is an honest Israelite. I hope You will meet him one day. I would like to take You to him. '

'That is quite possible. '

Judas joins in the conversation: 'Master, You promised to come with me, in Judaea. '

'And I will. Simon will continue to teach the people on My coming. The time is short, My dear friends, and the people are so many. I will now go with Simon. You two will come and meet Me this evening on the road to the Mount of Olives and we will give money to the poor. Go now. '

When Jesus is alone with Simon, He asks him: 'Is that person in Bethany a true Israelite? '

'He is a true Israelite. His ideas are the prevailing ones, but he is really longing for the Messiah. And when I said to him: "He is now among us", he replied at once: "I am blessed because I am living this hour." '

'We shall go to him one day and take our blessing to his house. Have you seen the new disciple? '

'I have. He is young and seems intelligent. '

'Yes, he is. Since you are a Judaean, You will bear more with him than the others will, because of his ideas. '

'Is that a desire, or an order? '

'A kind order. You have suffered and You can be more indulgent. Sorrow teaches many things. '

'If You give me an order, I will be totally indulgent to him. '

'Yes. Be so. Perhaps Peter, and he may not be the only one, will be somewhat upset seeing how I take care and worry about this disciple. But one day, they will understand... The more one is deformed, the more assistance one needs.

The others... oh! The others form properly, also by themselves, by simple contact. I do not want to do everything by Myself. I want the will of man and the help of other people to form a man. I ask you to help Me... and I am grateful for the help. '

'Master do You think he will disappoint You? '

'No. But he is young and was brought up in Jerusalem. '

'Oh! near You he will amend all the vices of that town... I am sure. I was already old and hardened by bitter hatred, and yet I have changed completely after seeing You... '

Jesus whispers: 'So be it! 'Then in a loud voice: 'Let us go to the Temple. I will evangelize the people. '

Jesus, John, Simon And Judas Go To Bethlehem.

Jesus, Who is already with John, meets Simon and Judas, early in the morning, at the same gate in Jerusalem.

'My friends...' says Jesus '...I ask you to come with Me through Judaea. If it is not too much for you, particularly for you, Simon.'
'Why, Master?'
'It is hard to walk on the Judaean mountains... and perhaps it will be even more painful for you to meet someone who harmed you.'
'As far as the road is concerned, I wish to assure You, once again, that since You cured me, I feel stronger than a young man and no work is heavy for me, also because it is done for You, and now, with You. With regard to meeting people who harmed me, there is no harsh resentment or feeling in Simon's heart, since he became Yours. Hatred has gone together with the scales of the disease. And believe me, I cannot tell You whether You worked a greater miracle in curing my corroded flesh or my soul consumed by hatred. I do not think I am wrong in saying the curing my soul was the greater miracle; A wound of the soul heals less easily... and You cured me in one instant. That is a miracle. Because one does not recover all of a sudden, even if one wants to with

all of one's strength and a man does not get rid of
a bad moral habit, if You do not destroy that habit
with Your sanctifying will power.'
'Your judgment is correct.'
'Why do You not do that with everyone? ' asks
Judas, somewhat resentfully.
'But He does, Judas...' put in John, laying a kind
and loving arm on Judas as though to calm him
down and speaking anxiously and persuasively '...
Why do you speak like that to the Master? Do you
not feel you have changed since you have been in
contact with Him? Previously, I was a disciple of
John the Baptist. But I have found myself
completely changed since He said to me: "Come".'

John, who seldom interferes, and never does in the presence of the Master, finds himself compelled to speak but then realises he has spoken before Jesus, blushes and says:

'Forgive me, Master, I spoke in Your stead, but I wanted... I did not want Judas to grieve You.'

'Yes, John. But he did not grieve Me as My disciple. When he is My disciple, then, if he persists in his way of thinking, he will grieve Me. It grieves Me only to notice how much man has been corrupted by Satan who perverts his thoughts. All men, you know! The thoughts of all of you have been misled by him! But the day will come, when you will have the Strength and the Grace of God, you will have Wisdom with His Spirit... you will then have everything to enable you to judge rightly.'

'And will we all judge rightly.'

'No, Judas.'

'But are You referring to us, disciples, or to all men?'

'I refer firstly to you, and to all the others. When the time comes, the Master will nominate His workers and send them all over the world...'

'Are You not doing that already?'

'For the time being, I use you only to say: "The Messiah is here. Come to Him." Later I will make you capable of preaching in My name, of working miracles in My name...'

'Oh! Also miracles?'

'Yes, on bodies and on souls.'

'Oh! How they will admire us, then! ' exhales Judas, overjoyed at the thought.

'But, then, we shall not be with the Master... and I will always be afraid to do with my human capacity what comes only from God ' says John, looking thoughtfully and somewhat sadly at Jesus.

'John, if the Master will allow me, I would like to

tell you what I think ' says Simon.

'Yes, tell John. I want you to advise one another.'

'Do You already know it is advice?' Jesus smiles and is quiet.

'Well, I tell you, John, that you must not, we must not be afraid. Let us found upon His wisdom of a holy Master and upon His promise. If He says: "I will send you", it means that He knows that He can send us without any fear that we may do harm to Him or to ourselves, that is to the cause of God, that is so dear to each of us, like a newly-wed bride. If He promises to clothe our intellectual and spiritual misery with the brightness of the power His Father gives Him for us, we must be certain that He will do so and that we will be successful, not by ourselves, but through His mercy. All this will most certainly happen, providing our deeds are free from pride and human ambitions. I think that if we contaminate our mission, which is entirely a spiritual one, with earthly ingredients, then also Christ's promise will no longer stand. Not because of any inability on His part, but because we will strangle such ability with the rope of pride. I do not know whether I have made myself understood.'

'You have spoken very clearly. I am wrong. But you know... I think that after all, to wish to be admired as the Messiah's disciples, so close to Him as to deserve to do what He does, is the same as wishing to increase even more the powerful figure of Christ among people. Praise to the Master, Who has such disciples, that is what I mean' answers Judas.

'What you say is not entirely wrong. But... see, Judas. I come from a caste which is persecuted because... because it misunderstood what and how the Messiah should be. Yes. If we had waited for Him with the correct vision of His being, we would not have fallen into errors, which blaspheme against the Truth and rebel against the Law of Rome, so that we have been punished both by God

and by Rome. We fancied Christ as a conqueror who would free Israel, as a new Maccabaeus, greater than the great Judas... Only that. And why? Because rather than have regard to the interest of God we took care of our own interests: of the fatherland and of the people. Oh! The interests of the fatherland are most certainly sacred. But what are they when compared to the eternal Heavens? In the long hours of persecution, first, and then of isolation, when as a fugitive, I was compelled to hide in the dens of wild beasts, sharing food and bed with them, to escape Roman power and above all the impeachments of false friends; or when, whilst waiting for death in the cave of a leper, I already had a foretaste of the savour of the sepulchre, how much did I meditate, and how much did I see: I saw the figure of the Messiah... Yours, my humble and good Master, Yours, Master and King of the Spirit, Yours, O Christ, Son of the Father, leading to the Father, and not to the royal palaces of dust, nor to the deities of mud. You... Oh! It is easy for me to follow You... Because, forgive my daring which avows itself to be correct, because I see You as I thought of You, I recognise You, I recognised You at once. No, it was not a question of meeting You, but of recognising One whom my soul had already met...'
'That is why I called you... and that is why I am taking you with Me, now, in this first journey of Mine in Judaea. I want you to complete your recognition... and I want also these, whom age makes less capable of reaching the Truth by means of deep meditation, I want them to know how their Master has come to this hour... You will understand later. There is David's Tower. The Eastern Gate is near.'
'Are we going out by it?'
'Yes, Judas. We are going to Bethlehem first. Where I was born... You ought to know... to tell the

others. Also that is part of the knowledge of the
Messiah and of the Scriptures. You will find
prophecies written in things not as prophecies but
as history. Let us go round Herod's houses...'
'The old, wicked, lustful fox.'
'Do not judge. There is God, Who judges. Let us go
along the path through these vegetable gardens.
We will stop under the shade of a tree, near some
hospitable house, until it cools down. Then we will
go on our way.'

Jesus At Bethlehem In The Peasant's House And In The Grotto.

It is a hot dry summer day on a flat road covered in dust and stones, running along an Olive grove of huge olive trees laden with small newly formed olives. Where it has not been trodden, the ground is strewn with minute olive flowers shaken to the ground during pollination.

Keeping in the shade of the olive trees and away from the worst of the dust, Jesus with His three disciples proceed in a single along the edge of the road where the grass is still green, following it as it turns in a right angle where there is a closed and abandoned square building surmounted by a little low dome. From there, it is an easy climb into a large horseshoe shaped valley strewn with houses forming a small town.

'That is Rachel's sepulchre' says Simon.

'In that case, we have almost arrived. Are we going into town at once?'

'No, Judas, I want to show you a place first... Then we will go into town, and since there is still clear daylight and it will be an evening of moonlight, we will be able to speak to the people. If they will listen to us.'

'Do You think they will not listen to You?'

They reach the sepulchre, an ancient whitewashed

and well-preserved monument.

Jesus stops to drink at a rustic well nearby. A woman who has come to draw water offers Him some.

'Are you from Bethlehem?' Jesus asks her.

'I am. But now at harvest time, I live in the country here with my husband, to look after the vegetable gardens and the orchards. Are You Galilean?'

'I was born in Bethlehem, but I live at Nazareth in Galilee.'

'Are You persecuted, too?'

'The family is. But why do you say: "You too"? Are there many people persecuted among the Bethlehemites?'

'Don't You know? What age are You?'

'Thirty.'

'Then You were born exactly when... oh! what a calamity! But why was He born here?'

'Who?'

'The One they said was the Saviour. Cursed be the fools who, drunk as they were, thought the clouds were angels and the bleating and braying were voices from Heaven, and in their drunken haze mistook three miserable people for the holiest people on the earth. Cursed be they! And cursed be those who believe them.'

'But, with all your cursing, you are not telling Me what happened. Why are you cursing?'

'Because... Listen: where are You going?'

'To Bethlehem with My friends. I have business there. I must visit some old friends and take them the greetings of My Mother. But I would like to know many things before, because we have been away, we of the family, for many years. We left the town when I was only a few months old.'

'Before the catastrophe, then. Listen, if You do not loathe the house of a peasant, come and share our bread and salt with us. You and Your companions. We will talk during supper and I will put you all up for the night. My house is small. But above the stable there is a lot of hay, all piled up. The night is clear and warm. If You want, You can sleep there.'

'May the Lord of Israel reward your hospitality. I will be happy to come to your house.'

'A pilgrim brings blessings with him. Let us go. But I shall have to pour six jars of water on the vegetables which have just come up.'

'And I will help you.'

'No, You are a gentleman, Your behaviour says so.'

'I am a worker, woman. This one is a fisherman. Those two Judaeans are well off and employed. I am not.' And He picks up a jar which was lying flat on its big belly near the very low wall of the well, He ties it to the rope, and lowers it into the well. John helps Him. Also the others wish to be as helpful and they ask the woman: ' Where are the vegetables? Tell us and we will take the jars there.'

'May God bless you! My back is broken with fatigue. Come...'

And while Jesus is pulling up His jar, the three disciples disappear along a little path... and come back with two empty ones, which they fill up and then go away. And they do not do that three, but ten times. And Judas laughing says: ' She is shouting herself hoarse, blessing us. We have given so much water to her salad that the soil will be damp for at least two days, and the woman will not have to break her back. '

When he comes back for the last time, he says:
'Master, I am afraid we have been unlucky.'
'Why, Judas?'
'Because she has it in for the Messiah. I said to
her: "Don't curse. Don't you know that the Messiah
is the greatest grace for the people of God? Yahweh
promised Him to Jacob, and after him to all the
Prophets and the just people in Israel. And you
hate Him?" She replied: "Not Him. But the one
whom some drunken shepherds and three cursed

diviners from the East called 'Messiah' ". And since that is You...'

'It does not matter. I know I am placed as a trial and contradiction for many. Did you tell her who I am?'

'No, I am not a fool. I wanted to save Your back and ours.'

'You did well. Not because of our backs. But because I wish to show Myself when I think the time is right. Let us go.'

Judas leads Him as far as the vegetable garden.

The woman empties the last three jars and then takes Him towards a rustic building in the middle of the orchard. 'Go in' she says. 'My husband is already in the house.'

They look into a low smoky kitchen. ' Peace be to this house ' greets Jesus.

'Whoever You are, may You and Your friends be blessed. Come in' replies the man. And he takes a basin of water out to them to refresh and clean themselves after which they all go in and sit round a rough table.

'Thank you for helping my wife. She told me. I had never dealt with Galileans before and I was told that they are rough and quarrelsome. But you have been kind and good. Although already tired... you worked so hard. Are you coming from far?'

'From Jerusalem. These two are Judaeans. The other one and I are from Galilee. But, believe Me, man: you will find good and bad everywhere.'

'That's true. I, the first time I have met Galileans, I have found them to be good. Woman: bring the food. I have but bread, vegetables, olives and cheese. I am a peasant.'

'I am not a gentleman Myself. I am a carpenter.'

'What? You? With Your manners?'

The woman intervenes: 'Our guest is from Bethlehem, I told you, and if His relations are persecuted, they were probably rich and learned, like Joshua of Ur, Matthew of Isaac, Levi of Abraham, poor people!...‘

'You have not been questioned. Forgive her. Women are more talkative than sparrows in the evening.‘

'Were they Bethlehemite families?‘

'What? You do not know who they are, and You come from Bethlehem?‘

'We ran away when I was a few months old...‘ but the talkative woman interrupts 'He went away before the massacre.‘

'Eh! I see that. Otherwise He would not be in this world. Have You never been back?‘

'No, never.‘

'What a calamity! You will not find many of those Sarah said You want to meet and visit. Many were killed, many ran away, many... who knows!... missing, and it has never been known whether they died in the desert or were killed in jail as a punishment for their rebellion. But was it a rebellion? And who would have remained inactive allowing so many innocents to be slaughtered? No, it is unfair that Levi and Elias should still be alive when so many innocents are dead!‘

'Who are those two, and what did they do?‘

'Well... at least You will have heard of the slaughter. The slaughter by Herod... Over a thousand babies slaughtered in town, almost another thousand in the country (1). And they were all, or almost all, males, because in their fury, in the darkness, in the scuffle, the killers tore away from their cradles, from their mother's beds, from the houses they assailed, also some baby girls, and they pierced them like sucking baby gazelles shot down by archers. Well: why all that? Because a group of shepherds, who had obviously drank a huge quantity of cider to withstand the intense night cold, in a frenzy of excitement, stated they had seen angels, heard songs, received instructions... and they said to us of Bethlehem: "Come. Adore. The Messiah is born." Just imagine: the Messiah in a cave! In all sincerity, I must admit that we were all drunk, even I, then an adolescent, also my wife, then only a few years old... because we all believed them, and in a poor Galilean woman we saw the Virgin Mother mentioned by the Prophets. But She was with Her husband, a rough Galilean! If She was the wife, how could She be the "Virgin"? To cut a long story short: we believed.

Gifts, worshipping... houses opened to give them hospitality!...

Oh! They played their roles very well! Poor Anne! She lost her property and her life, and also the children of her oldest daughter, the only one left because she was married to a merchant in Jerusalem, lost all their property because their house was burned down and the whole holding was laid waste by Herod's order. Now it is an uncultivated field where herds feed.'

'And was it entirely the shepherds' fault?'

'No, it was the fault also of three wizards who came from Satan's kingdom. Perhaps they were accomplices of the three... And we foolishly felt proud of so much honour! And the poor arch synagogue! We killed him because he swore that the prophecies confirmed the truth of the shepherds' and wizards' words...'

'It was therefore the fault of the shepherds and of the wizards?'

'No, Galilean. It was also our fault. The fault of our credulity. The Messiah had been expected for such a long time! Centuries of expectation. And there had been many recent disappointments because of false Messiahs. One of them was a Galilean, like You, another one was named Theudas. Liars! They... Messiahs! They were nothing but greedy adventurers hunting for a stroke of luck! We should have learned the lesson. Instead...'

'Well, then, why do you curse all the shepherds and magicians? If you consider yourselves fools, too, then you ought to be cursed as well. But the precept of love forbids cursing. One curse attracts another curse. Are you sure you are right? Could it not be true that the shepherds and the magicians spoke the truth, revealed to them by God? Why do you persist in believing they were liars?'

'Because the years of the prophecy were not complete. We thought about it afterwards... after our eyes had been opened by the blood that reddened basins and rivulets.'

'And could the Most High not have advanced the coming of the Saviour, out of an excess of love for His people? On what did the wizards found their statement? You told Me they came from the East...'

'On their calculations concerning a new star.'

'Is it not written: "A star from Jacob takes the leadership, a sceptre arises from Israel"? Is Jacob not the great Patriarch and did he not stop in the land of Bethlehem as dear to him as his eyes, because his beloved Rachel died there?

And did the mouth of a Prophet not say: "A shoot springs from the stock of Jesse, a scion thrusts from his roots"? Jesse, David's father, was born here. Is the shoot on the stock, cut at its roots by tyrannical usurpations, is it not the "Virgin" Who will give birth to Her Son, conceived not by deed of man, otherwise She would not be a virgin, but by divine will, whereby He will be the "Immanuel" because: Son of God, He will be God and bring God among the people of God, as His name proclaims? And will He not be announced, as the prophecy says, to the people walking in darkness, that is to the heathens, "by a great light"? And the star the magicians saw, could it not be the star of Jacob, the great light of the two prophecies of

91

Balaam and Isaiah? And the very massacre ordered by Herod, does it not come within the prophecies? "A voice is heard in Ramah... It is Rachel weeping for her children." It was written that tears should ooze from Rachel's bones in her sepulchre at Ephrathah when, through the Saviour, the reward would come to the holy people. Tears which were to turn into celestial laughter, just as the rainbow is formed by the last drops of the storm, but it says: "Here, the sky is clear."'

'You are a learned man. Are You a rabbi?'

'Yes, I am.'

'And I perceived it. There is light and truth in Your words. But... Oh! too many wounds are still bleeding in this land of Bethlehem because of the true or false Messiah... I would never advise Him to come here. The land would reject Him as it rejects a stepson who caused the death of the true children. In any case... if it was Him... He died with the other slaughtered children.'

'Where do Levi and Elias live now?'

'Do You know them?' The man becomes suspicious.

'I do not know them. Their faces are unknown to Me. But they are unhappy, and I always have mercy on the unhappy. I want to go and see them.'

'Well, You will be the first one after about thirty years. They are still shepherds and they work for a rich Herodian from Jerusalem, who has taken possession of a lot of the property belonging to the people killed... There is always someone making a profit! You will find them with their herds on the high grounds towards Hebron. But this is my advice: don't let anyone from Bethlehem see You speaking to them. You would suffer from it. We bear them because... because of the Herodian. Otherwise...'

'Oh! Hatred! Why hate?'

'Because it is just. They have done us harm.'

'They thought they were doing good.'
'But they did harm. Let them be harmed. We should have killed them as they had so many people killed through their stupidity. But we had become stupid ourselves and later... there was the Herodian.'
'So, even if he had not been there, after the first desire for revenge, which was still excusable, would you have killed them?'
'We would kill them even now, if we were not afraid of their master.'
'Man, I tell you, do not hate. Do not wish evil things. Do not be anxious to do evil things. There is no fault here. But even if there was, forgive. Forgive in the name of God. Tell the other people of Bethlehem as well. When your hearts are free from hatred, the Messiah will come; you will know Him then, because He is alive. He already existed when the massacre took place. I am telling you. It was Satan's fault, not the fault of the shepherds and of the magicians that the massacre took place. The Messiah was born here for you, He came to bring the Light to the land of His fathers. The Son of a Virgin Mother of the line of David, in the ruins of the house of David, He granted a stream of Graces to the world, and a new life to mankind...'
'Go away! Get out of here! You are a follower of that false Messiah, Who could but be false, because He brought misfortune to us here in Bethlehem. You are defending Him, so...'
'Be silent, man. I am a Judaean and I have influential friends. I could make you feel sorry for your insult' bursts out Judas, getting hold of the peasant's garments, and shaking him in a fit of violent anger.
'No, No, out of here! I don't want trouble with the people of Bethlehem or with Rome or Herod. Go away, you cursed ones, if you don't want me to leave my mark on you... Out!'

'Let us go, Judas. Do not react. Let us leave him in his hatred. God will not enter where there is bitter hatred. Let us go.'

'Yes, we will go. But you will pay for it.'

'No, Judas, do not say that. They are blind... We shall meet so many on My way.'

They go out and find Simon and John, who are outside, speaking to the woman, round the comer of the stable.

'Forgive my husband, Lord. I did not think I was going to cause so much trouble... Here, take these-' She gives Him some eggs- 'You will eat them tomorrow morning. They are newly laid. I have nothing else... Forgive us. Where will You sleep?'

'Do not worry. I know where to go. Go and peace be with you for your kindness. Goodbye.'

They walk a short distance, without speaking, then Judas bursts out: 'But You... Why not make him worship You? Why did You not crush that filthy swearer down in the mud? Down on the ground! Crushed because he showed no respect for You, the Messiah... Oh! That is what I would have done! Samaritans should be reduced to ashes by means of a miracle! It is the only thing that will shake them.'

'Oh! How many times will I hear that said! But if I should reduce to ashes for every sin against Me!... No, Judas. I have come to create, not to destroy.'

'Yes! And in the meantime they are destroying You.' Jesus does not reply.

Simon asks: ' Where are we going now, Master?'

'Come with Me, I know a place.'

'But if You have never been here after You left, how can You know?' asks Judas, still angry.

'I know. It is not a beautiful place. But I have been there before. It is not in Bethlehem... it is a little outside... Let us turn this way.'

Jesus is in front, followed by Simon, then Judas and John is last... In the silence, broken only by the rustling of their sandals on the small grains of gravel of the path, the sounds of sobbing can be heard.

'Who is crying?' asks Jesus turning round.

'It's John. He has been frightened.' answers Judas.

'No, I was not frightened. I had already laid my hand on the knife under my belt... Then I remembered the words You keep repeating: "Do not kill, forgive."'

'Why are you crying, then?' asks Judas.

'Because I suffer seeing that the world does not love Jesus. They do not know Him, and they do not want to know Him. Oh! It is such a pain! As if someone tore my heart with burning thorns. As if I had seen someone treading on my mother or spitting upon my father's face... Even worse... As if I had seen Roman horses eating in the Holy Ark and resting in the Holy of Holies.'

'Do not cry, My dear John. Say for this present time and for endless times in future: "He was the Light and He came to enlighten darkness – but darkness did not know Him. He came to the world that had been made for Him, but the world did not know Him. He came to His own town, to His domain, but His own people did not accept Him." Oh! Do not cry like that!'

'That does not happen in Galilee!' says John sighing.

'Well, not even in Judaea ' says Judas.' Jerusalem is the capital and three days ago it sang hosannas to You, Messiah! You cannot judge from this place of coarse peasants, shepherds and market gardeners. Also the Galileans, mind you, are not all good. After all, where did Judas, the false Messiah, come from? They said...'

'That is enough, Judas. There is no use in getting angry. I am calm. Be calm, too. Judas, come here. I want to speak to you. ' Judas goes near Him.' Take this purse. You will do the shopping for

tomorrow.'
'And for the time being, where are we going to lodge?'
Jesus smiles, but does not reply.

It is dark and the vault of heaven is strewn with stars, stars stars as on a heavenly curtain, a canopy of living gems spread over the hills of Bethlehem awash in the also in the moonlight that turns everything white. Nightingales are singing in the olives trees . Nearby, the silvery ribbon of a brook, bellows Oxen and bleatings of sheep. The air is perfumed with the smell of toasted hay of the mown fields.

'But here!... There is nothing but ruins here! Where are You taking us? The town is over there.'
'I know. Come. Follow the rivulet, behind Me. A few more steps and then... then I will offer you the abode of the King of Israel.'
Judas shrugs and becomes quiet.
A few more steps, then a heap of ruined houses: the remains of houses... A cave between the clefts of a big wall.

Jesus asks: ' Have You any tinder? Light it.'
Simon lights a small lamp which he has taken out of his knapsack and gives it to Jesus.
'Come in ' says the Master lifting the lamp. 'Come in. This is the nativity room of the King of Israel.'
'You must be joking, Master! This is a filthy den. Ah! I am not going to stay here! I loathe it: it is damp, cold, stinking, full of scorpions and perhaps also snakes...'
'And yet... My friends, here the night of the twenty-fifth of Chislev, Feast of the Lights, Jesus Christ, was born of the Virgin, the Immanuel, the Word of God made flesh, for the love of man: I Who am speaking to you. Also then, as now, the world was

deaf to the voices of Heaven speaking to the hearts
of men... and it rejected the Mother... and here...
No, Judas, do not avert your eyes in disgust from
those fluttering bats, from those green lizards,
from those cobwebs, do not lift with disgust your
beautiful embroidered mantle, lest it trail on the
ground covered with animal excrement. Those bats
are the grand daughters of the ones that were the
first toys to be tossed before the eyes of the Child,
for Whom the angels sang the "Gloria" heard by
the shepherds, intoxicated only by an ecstatic joy,
a true joy. The emerald green of those lizards was
the first colour to strike My eyes, the first, after My
Mother's white face and dress. Those cobwebs were
the canopy of My royal cradle. This ground... oh!
you may tread on it without disdain... It is littered
with excrement... but it is sanctified by Her foot,
the foot of the Holy, the Most Holy, Pure,
Immaculate Mother of God, Who gave birth,
because She was to give birth, because God, not
man, told Her and covered Her with His shadow.
She, the Faultless One, trod on it. You can tread
on it, too. And may the purity diffused by Her, by
the will of God, rise from the soles of your feet to
your heart...'
Simon is on his knees. John goes straight to the
manger and cries, leaning his head against it.
Judas is terrified... he is overcome by emotion, and
no longer worried about his beautiful mantle, he
kneels on the ground, takes the edge of Jesus'
tunic and kisses it and beats his breast saying:
'Oh! My good Master, have mercy on the blindness
of Your servant! My pride vanishes... I see You as
You are. Not the king I was thinking of. But the
Eternal Prince, the Father of future centuries, the
King of peace. Have mercy, my Lord and my God,
have mercy on me!'

'Yes, you have all My mercy! Now we will sleep

where the Infant and the Virgin slept, over there where John has taken the place of the adoring Mother, here where Simon looks like My putative father. Or, if you prefer so, I will speak to you of that night...'

'Oh! yes, Master, tell us of Your birth.'

'That it may be a bright pearl shining in our hearts. And we may tell the whole world.'

'And we may venerate Your Virgin Mother, not only as Your Mother, but also as... as the Virgin!'

Judas was the first to speak, then Simon and then John, whose face smiles and cries, near the manger.

'Come and sit on the hay. Listen... ' and Jesus tells them of the night of His birth.' ... as the Mother was near Her time to have Her Child, a decree was issued by the imperial delegate Publius Sulpicius Quirinus on instructions from Caesar Augustus, when Sentius Saturninus was governor of Palestine. The decree stated that a census had to be taken of all the people of the empire. Those who were not slaves were to go to their places of origin and register in the official rolls of the empire. Joseph, the spouse of the Mother, was of the line of David and the Mother was also of David's line. In compliance with the decree, they left Nazareth and came to Bethlehem, the cradle of the royal family. The weather was severe...'

END

If you enjoyed this book, please kindly submit a review. Thank you!

Next in Series

Those Who are Marked

....

Judas, Simon and John are with Jesus and they are walking through a valley between two mountain chains. They have left the shepherds behind, in the pastures of Hebron. The fields in this valley are not very large, but they are well cultivated with various cereals, mainly barley and rye and also some nice vineyards in the sunny parts. Higher up, there are lovely forests of Pine trees, fir trees and other trees typical of woody forests. A reasonably good road leads into a small village.

'This is the suburb of Kerioth. Please come to my country house. My mother is waiting for You there. We will go to Kerioth afterwards 'says Judas who is beside himself with excitement.

'As you wish, Judas, but we could have stopped even here to meet your mother. '

'Oh! No! It is only a farm house. My mother comes here at harvest time. But she lives in Kerioth. And do You not want my town people to see You? Do You not want to take Your light to them? '

'I certainly do, Judas. But you already are aware that I do not mind the humility of the place that gives Me hospitality. '

'But today You are my guest... and Judas knows how to be hospitable. '

They walk for a few more yards among houses spread about the country; men and women look out and children call, their curiosity awakened. Judas must have sent word to warn them.

'Here is my poor house. Forgive its poverty. '

But, the house is neither small nor squalid nor simply constructed. It consists of a large well-kept ground floor in the middle of a thick flowering orchard via a small clean private road leading from the main road to the house.

'May I go ahead of You, Master? '

'Yes, go. 'Judas goes.

'Master, Judas has done things in great style 'says Simon, 'I rather suspected he would. But now I am certain. Master, You keep saying, and quite rightly, spirit... But he... he does not see things that way. He will never understand You... or perhaps only very late 'he adds not to grieve Jesus. Jesus sighs and is silent.

Judas comes out with a woman of about fifty years old, rather tall, but not so tall as her son, who has her dark eyes and curly hair. But her eyes are kind and rather sad, whereas those of Judas are imperious and shrewd.

'I greet You, King of Israel 'she says prostrating herself in a real salutation of a subject. 'Allow Your servant to give You hospitality. '

'Peace to you, woman. And may God be with you and your creature. '

'Oh! yes! With my creature. 'She sighs.

'Stand up, mother. I have a Mother, too, and I cannot allow you to kiss My feet. I kiss you, woman, in My Mother's name. She is a sister of yours... in love and in the painful destiny of the mother of those who are marked. '

'What do You mean, Messiah? 'Asks Judas somewhat worried.

But Jesus does not reply. He is embracing the woman, whom He has kindly raised up from the ground and is now kissing her cheeks. And, holding her hand, He walks toward the house.

They go into a cool room, shaded by light striped curtains. Cold drinks and fresh fruit are already laid out. But first, Judas' mother calls a maidservant who brings in water and the landlady would like to take off Jesus' sandals and wash His dusty feet. But Jesus objects. 'No, mother. A mother is too holy a person, particularly when she is honest and good, as you are, to be allowed to take the attitude of a slave... '

The mother looks at Judas... an unusual look and then she goes away.

Jesus has refreshes Himself. When He is about to put on His sandals, the woman comes back with a new pair. 'Here, Messiah. I think I have done the right thing... as Judas wanted... He said to me: "A little longer than mine, but the same width."'

'But why, Judas? '

'Will You not let me offer You a gift? Are You not my King and my God? '

'Yes, Judas. But you must not give so much trouble to your mother. You know what I am like... '

'I know. You are holy. But You must appear as a holy King. That is how one imposes oneself. – In the world, where nine tenths of the folk are foolish people, we must impose ourselves with our appearance. Trust me. '

Jesus has fastened the red leather open-work straps of the new sandals, which reach up to His ankles. They are much nicer than His plain sandals of a workman, and they resemble Judas' sandals, which are like shoes with open- work showing parts of his feet.

'Also the tunic, my King. I prepared it for Judas... But he makes a present of it to You. It's a linen one: cool and new. Allow a mother to put it on You... as if You were her son. '

Jesus looks at Judas once again... but does not speak. He unties the lace of His tunic, round His neck, and lets His wide tunic fall on to the floor and thus is left with only His short under-tunic. The woman puts on Him the lovely new garment. And then offers Him a richly embroidered braided belt with a hanging cord decorated with very thick tassels. Jesus must feel comfortable in the cool clean clothes, but He does not seem very happy. In the meantime the others have cleaned themselves.

'Come, Master. They come from my poor orchard. And this is honeyed water, prepared by my mother. Perhaps, Simon, you would prefer this white wine.

Have some. It is the wine of my vineyard. And what about you, John? Will you have the same as the Master? 'Judas is overjoyed as he pours the drinks into beautiful silver cups, thus showing his wealth.

His mother is not very talkative. She looks... looks... at Judas, and even more at Jesus, and when Jesus, before eating, offers her the nicest fruit-yellow red in colour- and He says to her:

'First of all to mother, always ', her eyes well with tears.

'Mother, is the rest ready? 'Asks Judas.

'Yes, son. I think I have done everything well. But I was brought up here and I have always lived here and I do not know... I do not know the habits of kings. '

'Which habits, woman? Which kings? What have You done, Judas? '

'Are You not the promised King of Israel? It is time that the world should salute You as such, and that must happen for the first time here, in my town, in my house. I revere You as such. For my sake, and for the respect due to Your names of Messiah, Christ, King, which the Prophets gave You by Yahweh's command, do not give me the lie. '

'Woman, friends, please. I must speak to Judas. I have precise instructions to give him. '

The mother and the disciples withdraw.

'Judas: what have you done? Have you understood so little of Me so far? Why lower Me to the extent of making Me only a mighty man of the world, nay: a man intriguing to become mighty? And do you not understand that that is an offence, nay an obstacle to My mission? Yes. Do not deny it. It is an obstacle. Israel is subjected to Rome. You know what happened when they raised against Rome someone who seemed a mob-leader and aroused the suspicion of creating an insurrection. Only a few days ago you heard how pitiless they were against a Child because they were afraid He might be a king according to the world. And yet you!...

Oh! Judas! What do you expect from the sovereignty of the flesh? What do you expect? I gave you time to think and decide. I spoke to you very clearly from the very first time. I also sent you away because I knew... because I know, I read and see what is in you. Why do you want to follow Me, if you do not want to be as I want you? Go away, Judas. Do not harm yourself and do not harm Me... Go away. It is better for you. You are not a suitable worker for this task. It is by far too much above you. In you there is pride, there is greed and all its three branches, there is arrogance... even your mother must be afraid of you... you are inclined to falsehood... No, My follower must not be like that. Judas, I do not hate you, I do not curse you. I only say to you, and I am saying it with the grief of one who knows he cannot change the person he loves, I only say to you: go your way, make your way in the world, since that is what you want, but do not stay with Me.

My life!... My royal palace! How small and mean they are! Do you know where I will be a King? When I will be proclaimed King? When I will be raised up, upon an ill-famed piece of wood and My own blood will be My purple, and My crown will be a wreath of thorns and My insignia a mocking poster and the curses of all the people, of My people, will be the trumpets, the tambourines, the organs, the citherns saluting the proclamation of the King. And do you know by whose deed all this will happen? By the deed of one who did not understand Me. One who will have understood nothing. One, whose heart was a hollow piece of bronze, which pride, sensuality and avarice had filled with their humours, which will generate coils of snakes that will be used to chain Me and... and to curse him. The others are not so well aware of My destiny. Please do not tell them. Let us keep this to ourselves. In any case it is a reproach... and you will keep quiet to avoid saying: "I was reproached"... Is that clear, Judas? '

Judas has blushed so much, that he looks purple. He is standing before Jesus, mortified, his head lowered... He kneels down and he cries with his head on Jesus' knees: 'I love you, Master, Don't reject me. Yes, I am proud and foolish but don't send me away. No. Master. I will never do it again. You are right. It was thoughtless of me. But there is some love in my mistake. I wanted to honour You... and I wanted the others to honour You as well... because I love You. You said so three days ago: "When you make a mistake without malice, out of ignorance, it is not an error, but an imperfect judgement: like the error of children, and

I am here to make adults of you." Here I am, here against Your knees... You said You would be a father to me... and I am here against Your knees as if they were my father's, and I ask You to forgive me, and to make an "adult" of me, a holy adult... Don't send me away, Jesus, Jesus, Jesus... Not everything is wicked in me. You know: I left everything for you and I have come. You are much more than the honours and victories I got serving other people. You are indeed the love of poor unhappy Judas who would like to give You nothing but joy, and is instead the cause of pain for You... '

'That is all right, Judas. I forgive you once again... 'Jesus looks tired... 'I forgive you, hoping... hoping that in future you will understand Me. '

'Yes, Master. But, now, do not give me the lie, otherwise I will be laughed at. Everybody in Kerioth knows that I was coming with David's Descendant, the King of Israel... and the town has made preparations to welcome You... I thought I was doing a good thing... showing You what one must do to be respected and obeyed... and I also wanted to show John and Simon, and through them, all the others who love You but treat You as their equal... Also my mother would be mocked at, as the mother of a mad liar. For her sake, my Lord... And I swear that I... '

'Do not swear to Me. Swear to yourself, if you can, that You will not commit such a sin again. For the sake of your mother and your fellow citizens I will not shame you by going away without stopping here. Stand up. '

'What will You tell the others? '

'The truth... '

'No, don't. '

'The truth: that I gave you instructions for today. It is always possible to tell the truth in a charitable way. Let us go. Call Your mother and the others. '

Jesus is rather severe. He smiles again only when Judas comes back with his mother and the disciples. The woman seems in great distress and she gazes at Jesus but gains confidence when she sees His kind disposition.

'Shall we go to Kerioth? I have rested and I wish to thank you, mother, for all your kindness. May Heaven reward you and grant rest and peace to your late husband, for all your charity to Me. '

The woman tries to kiss His hand, but Jesus caresses her head and thus prevents her from doing so.

'The wagon is ready, Master. Come. '

Outside, in fact, an ox cart is just arriving. It is a comfortable cart, on which they have placed cushions as seats and a red tent as a cover.

'Get on, Master. '

'Your mother, first. '

The woman gets on and then Jesus and the others.

'Sit here, Master. ' (Judas no longer calls Him king).

Jesus sits in front, and Judas sits beside Him. The woman and the disciples are behind. The man driving the cart goads the oxen walking beside them.

It is a short journey; a little over four hundred meters. The first houses of Kerioth are now visible and it looks like a decent little town. A little boy who was watching on the sunny road immediately dashes away. When the cart reaches the first houses, the notables and the people welcome Him; the houses are decorated with draperies and branches. The people shout with joy and bow deeply. Jesus, from the height of His shaking throne, can but greet them and bless them.

The cart moves on and after crossing a square it turns into a street and stops before a house where the door is already wide open and two or three women are waiting at the door. They stop and get off. 'My house is Yours, Master. '

'Peace to it, Judas. Peace and holiness. '

They go in. Beyond the hall there is a large room, with low divans and inlaid furniture. The notables of the place and other people go in with Jesus. There is a lot of bowing and curiosity: a showy joyfulness. An impressive elderly man delivers a speech:

'It is a great honour for the land of Kerioth to receive You, my Lord. A great fortune! A happy day! It is a great fortune to have You and to see that a son of Kerioth is Your friend and assistant. May he be blessed because he met You before everyone else! And may You be blessed ten times ten because you have revealed Yourself: You are the one Who has been expected for generations and generations. Speak, my Lord and King. Our hearts are anxious to hear Your word, just as the land parched by a fiery summer awaits the first soft showers in September. ' ...